# Trueman and the Arsonists

## Max Frisch

**in a new version by Simon Stephens,
with songs by Chris Thorpe**

T0021313

*methuen* | drama

LONDON • NEW YORK • OXFORD • NEW DELHI • SYDNEY

METHUEN DRAMA
Bloomsbury Publishing Plc
50 Bedford Square, London, WC1B 3DP, UK
1385 Broadway, New York, NY 10018, USA
29 Earlsfort Terrace, Dublin 2, Ireland

BLOOMSBURY, METHUEN DRAMA and the Methuen
Drama logo are trademarks of Bloomsbury Publishing Plc

*Biedermann und die Brandstifter* by Max Frisch © Suhrkamp Verlag AG Berlin

This adaptation first published in Great Britain 2023

Cover design © Mobius Industries

A catalogue record for this book is available from the British Library.

A catalog record for this book is available from the Library of Congress.

ISBN: PB: 978-1-3504-4641-0
ePDF: 978-1-3504-4642-7
eBook: 978-1-03504-4643-4

Series: Modern Plays

Typeset by Mark Heslington Ltd, Scarborough, North Yorkshire

To find out more about our authors and books visit
www.bloomsbury.com and sign up for our newsletters.

*Trueman and the Arsonists*, written by Max Frisch in a new version by Simon Stephens, with songs by Chris Thorpe, premiered at the Studio Theatre at the Roundhouse in London on 18 October 2023. It was produced by represent. (Guy Woolf, Creative Director; Frankie Parham, Producer; Katy Beechey, Executive Director; Andy Lennard, Founding Director and Executive Producer) and directed by Abigail Graham. The set and costumes were designed by Lizzy Leech; the lighting design was by Rajiv Pattani; the sound design was by Zac Gvi; the costume supervisor was Katie Kelson; the casting director was Sarah Leung; the assistant director was Jillian Feuerstein; the production manager was Sean Laing; the stage managers were Joanna Nead and Lily Brown. The cast was as follows:

| | |
|---|---|
| Trueman | **Adam Owers** |
| Bobsy | **Nadine Ivy Barr** |
| Anna | **Thara Schöön** |
| Smith | **Tommy Oldroyd** |
| Ironside | **Angela Jones** |
| Police Officer/Professor/Mrs Waits | **Charlotte O'Leary** |
| Chorus | **Aaron Douglas** |
| Chorus | **Lucy Yates** |

# represent.

# Trueman and the Arsonists

**Characters**

**Trueman**
**Bobsy**, *his wife*
**Anna**, *a maid*
**Smith**, *a fighter*
**Molly Ironside/The Visitor**, *a waiter*
**A Police Officer**
**A Professor**
**Mrs Waits**, *a widow*
**A Chorus of Firefighters**

*A living room*
*An attic*
*A cellar*

*The stage is pitch black.*

*Then a match is lit.*

*It lights up a face.*

*It's* **Trueman**. *He's lighting a cigarette.*

**Trueman**   You can't even have a smoke nowadays without imagining the whole city on fire.

It's awful.

**Trueman** *puts the cigarette out.*

*He disappears into the smoke and the blackness.*

*A fire brigade enters.*

*A* **Chorus**. *They are present on the stage throughout.*

*Somewhere in the distance a town clock strikes a quarter past the hour.*

*The* **Chorus** *steps to the front.*

**Chorus**

Ladies and gentlemen.

We are the guardians of your city.

We watch you at all times.

We listen to you at all times.

We are friendly at all times.

I mean. You pay our wages.

We are well equipped.

Well trained.

Well ready.

We creep around your house.

Deathly alert and innocently unexpecting at one and the very same time.

Sometimes we sit and rest our tired feet.

But we never sleep.

We never tire.

We're watching.

We're listening.

Until the things that seem hidden.

Are finally revealed.

Before it's far too late.

To put out the fires.

*The clock strikes half past the hour.*

NOT ALL FIRES ARE FATE

YES THE LIGHT-EN-ING STRIKE

AND VOLCANO EXIST

BUT THEY DON'T SPRING FROM HATE

OR THE SMOULDERING ANGER

WE CARRY BELOW

THAT'S THE FIRE THAT WE WATCH FOR

THE DULL HUMAN GLOW

WHICH, WHEN FED WITH THE FUEL

OF SIMPLISTIC IDEAS

BY THE ONES WHO MIGHT GAIN

FROM THE STOKING OF FEARS,

WILL EXPLODE INTO FLAME

AND THEN SPREAD ON THE WIND

UNTIL VIOLENCE IS DONE

IF WE START TO BELIEVE
THAT OUR DESTINY'S TIED
TO THE DICE THROW, THE NOD
OF PURE CHAOS AND CHANCE,
THEN PERHAPS WE DESERVE
THE DESTRUCTION THAT COMES
WHEN WE FAIL TO SEE FLAMES
CREEPING CLOSER TO HOME.
NOT ALL FIRES ARE FATE
WE MUST WATCH FOR THE FLAMES
OF THE ONES THAT ARE STARTED
BY MALICE, FOR GAIN.
NOT ALL FIRES ARE FATE
WE MUST WATCH FOR THE FLAMES
WE MUST WATCH FOR THE FLAMES
WE MUST WATCH FOR THE FLAMES.
YOU HAVE MADE IT OUR JOB
TO WATCH FOR THE FLAMES.
YOU HAVE MADE IT OUR JOB
TO WATCH FOR THE FLAMES.
THIS MUST BE DONE
MUST BE SEEN TO BE DONE
SO YOU KNOW IT IS DONE
MUST BE SEEN TO BE DONE
SO YOU CAN SLEEP SOUNDLY

AND KNOW IT IS DONE

AND PERHAPS THINGS STILL BURN

BUT YOU KNOW IT IS DONE.

*The tower clock strikes the hour.*

Our shift has started.

*The* **Chorus** *sits down while the hourly beat sounds:*

*Nine o'clock.*


**Scene One**

*The Living Room*

**Godfrey Trueman** *sits reading the news and smoking.*

**Anna** *brings him a bottle of wine.*

**Anna**   Mr Trueman?

*He says nothing.*

Mr Trueman?

*He closes the newspaper.*

**Trueman**   They should hang them. The lot of them. I've said that from the start, haven't I? There's been another fire. It's the same thing. Exactly the same thing. I'm telling you. There's a, a, a man. A door-to-door salesman. A catalogue delivery man. He settles down in his attic. Seems to be doing nothing. Apparently hurting nobody.

**Anna**   Mr Trueman.

**Trueman**   What?

**Anna**   He's still out there.

**Trueman**   Who is?

**Anna**   That man. He's been waiting to talk to you.

**Trueman**  Tell him I'm not here.

**Anna**  I did tell him that. I told him that an hour ago. He says he knows you. I can't just, like, throw him out.

**Trueman**  Why not?

**Anna**  Cos he's enormous.

**Trueman** *opens the bottle of wine. Mulls on this news.*

**Trueman**  Tell him he should come to the office tomorrow.

**Anna**  I told him that three times. He doesn't seem to care.

**Trueman**  Why not?

**Anna**  He's not here to sell you anything.

**Trueman**  Isn't he?

**Anna**  Humans, eh? They absolutely do my head in.

**Trueman** *smells the cork.*

**Trueman**  Tell him I'll throw him out the door myself unless he leaves right away.

*He fills his glass.*

Humans, indeed.

*He drinks the wine.*

Alright. Tell him to wait in the hallway. I'll come and see what he wants. If he tries to sell me anything, mind you. Anything. A life insurance policy. A political party to vote for. A kitchen bloody cloth. I tell you, Anna, I'm not a cruel man. I'm not inhumane. You know that of all people. But I do not allow these people into my home. I've told you that a hundred times. I don't care how big this house looks from the outside. I don't care. I don't care. You know where it leads to, don't you? These days.

**Anna** *goes to leave.*

*The stranger comes in before she can get out of the door.*

*He looks like a strange athlete.*

*He's huge.*

*His clothes are a mix of prison uniform and circus sideshow. His arms are heavily tattooed. His wrists are bandaged with leather.*

**Anna** *tries to leave as slowly as she can.*

*The stranger waits until* **Trueman** *has tasted his wine and turned to him.*

**Smith**    Mr Trueman.

**Trueman** *drops his cigarette in astonishment.*

**Smith**    You've dropped your cigarette.

*He picks up the cigarette and hands it back to him.*

**Trueman**    What the hell are you doing in here?

**Smith**    And a good evening to you too, Mr Trueman.

**Trueman**    I told her to tell you to wait out there. And then. What? You just come in?

**Smith**    My name is Joseph.

**Trueman**    You don't even knock?

**Smith**    Joseph Smith.

*A silence for a time.*

It's lovely to meet you.

**Trueman**    What is it, precisely, that you want?

**Smith**    Mr Trueman, you don't need to worry. Don't be scared. I'm not here to sell you anything.

**Trueman**    Really?

**Smith**    I'm actually. I'm a fighter. By profession. A professional fighter.

**Trueman**    A fighter?

**Smith**    I'm a heavyweight.

**Trueman**    Excellent.

**Smith**    Or rather I used to be.

**Trueman**    And now you're – ?

**Smith**    I'm unemployed.

*There's a pause.*

Mr Trueman, you don't need to be frightened. I'm not looking for a job. I've given up fighting. I only came inside because it's raining outside.

*A pause.*

It's much warmer in here.

*A pause.*

I do hope I'm not annoying you.

*A pause.*

**Trueman**    Smoke?

**Trueman** *offers him a cigarette.*

**Smith**    It's terrible, Mr Trueman. For someone as huge as I am. Everyone's terrified of me.

*He takes the cigarette.*

Thank you.

**Trueman** *lights his cigarette for him.*

**Smith**    Thank you.

*They stand and smoke for a while.*

**Trueman**    So how exactly can I help you, Mr – ?

**Smith**    My name is Joseph Smith.

**Trueman**    Yes. You mentioned that. It's very nice to meet you, Mr Smith –

**Smith**   I'm homeless.

*He holds the cigarette in from of his nose and breathes in the smoke for a while.*

Homeless.

**Trueman**   Do you need some food? There's some bread . . .

**Smith**   Bread?

I mean if that's all you've got.

**Trueman**   I've got some wine.

**Smith**   Bread and wine. How very biblical. I don't want to bother you, Mr Trueman. I would hate to think of myself as a bother.

**Trueman** *goes to the door.*

**Trueman**   Anna!

*He comes back.*

**Smith**   She said to me, the girl did, she said that 'Mr Trueman wants to throw you out on your arse himself.' But I thought to myself, Mr Trueman, I thought you probably didn't mean that, did you?

**Anna** *enters.*

**Trueman**   Anna. Bring me another glass.

**Anna**   Straightaway, sir.

**Trueman**   And some bread. Yes. Bread.

**Smith**   And some butter. If you don't mind. And some cheese. Or some sliced ham.

Or something. Only if it's no bother. Some pickles. And a tomato. Or something. Some mustard. Whatever you've got really.

**Anna**   Right.

**Smith**   Only if it's no bother.

**Anna** *leaves.*

**Trueman**   She said you knew me.

**Smith**   I do, Mr Trueman. I do.

**Trueman**   How?

**Smith**   I only know your finer characteristics, Mr Trueman. I've only ever seen your good side. Last night. In the pub. I know you didn't notice me. I was slumped in the corner. The whole pub was so entertained by you, Mr Trueman. Every time you slammed your fist down on the bar. They all thought it was very funny.

**Trueman**   What was I talking about?

**Smith**   You were explaining what needed to be done about the arsonists.

*He smokes from his cigarette.*

'We should hang them. The lot of them. The sooner the better. Hang them all.'

**Trueman** *stands up. Offers a chair to* **Smith**.

**Trueman**   Please –

**Smith** *sits down.*

**Smith**   Men like you. Mr Trueman. That's what this city needs.

**Trueman**   Yes. I'm sure. But –

**Smith**   No buts, Mr Trueman. Don't give me a 'but'. Thing about you is you're old school. You have the right attitude. You have a positive attitude. That comes with it, I reckon.

**Trueman**   I'm sure.

**Smith**   You're fearless. You're committed to your whole society.

**Trueman**    Absolutely.

**Smith**    That comes with it, I reckon.

**Trueman**    With what, exactly?

**Smith**    You have a conscience. Still. Everyone in the whole bar could see it last night.

A real conscience.

**Trueman**    Well. Of course –

**Smith**    Mr Trueman, there's nothing of course about it. Not nowadays there's not. In the fight club where I used to fight, before that, you see, before that got burned down. The whole place! Our boss. He said to me. 'You tell me, Joe,' that's my name, Joe. Short for Joseph. 'You tell me,' he goes. 'Why should I live like I have a conscience. Really. You know what I need to manage this place? A fucking bullwhip.' Really! That's what he said. 'Conscience!' He's laughing! 'Anybody with a conscience. You look hard enough, Joe. They're the fucking guilty ones.'

*He smokes his cigarette with big deep happy sucks.*

God bless his soul.

**Trueman**    What? Is he dead?

**Smith**    Burned alive in the club with everything he ever owned.

*A clock strikes 9 pm.*

**Trueman**    What is taking that girl so long?

**Smith**    I'm not in any hurry.

*The two men look at one another for a while.*

Anyway. It's not like you've got a spare bed in the house, Mr Trueman. She told me that already.

**Trueman**    What are you laughing at?

**Smith**  'No spare bed.' 'No spare bed.' 'No spare bed.' It's what everybody says.

I'm a homeless person, Mr Trueman. I don't need a bed.

**Trueman**  Don't you?

**Smith**  I've got used to it. Mr Trueman. I sleep on the floor. My father worked at the incinerator of the power station. I've become immune.

*He takes another smoke and lets the smoke out into* **Mr Trueman***'s face.*

No buts. Mr Trueman. No buts. You know what I think? I think you're not one of those pricks who goes mouthing off in the pub because he's secretly absolutely terrified. I believe in you. 'There is, unfortunately, no spare bed in this whole house.' That's what everyone else says. But you, Mr Trueman. I believe you. Mr Trueman. I believe everything you say. What would happen if people stopped trusting each other? That's what I always say. What will it lead to, kids? Everybody has started to believe that everybody else is an arsonist. There is nothing but mistrust and suspicion in this world. Am I right or am I right? That's what everybody could see, last night, Mr Trueman. You still believe in people. You still believe in the good in people. You believe in the good in yourself. And in other people. Am I right or am I right? Or am I wrong? You are the first person in this city who hasn't just treated me like I'm a fucking arsonist.

**Trueman**  An ashtray?

**Smith**  Am I right or am I right?

*He tips fag ash into the ashtray.*

Most people don't even believe in God nowadays. But they do believe in the fire brigade.

**Trueman**  What do you mean?

**Smith**  It's true.

**Anna** *brings a tray in.*

**Anna**    We haven't got any ham.

**Smith**    Oh that's fine! Thank you. That's great. That's plenty. You forgot the mustard.

**Anna**    Sorry!

*She leaves.*

**Trueman**    Tuck in.

**Trueman** *fills their glasses.*

**Smith**    You don't get this kind of treatment everywhere you know, Mr Trueman. I'll tell you that for nothing. The things that have happened to me. As soon as I step through somebody's door. Because of the way I look. Because I'm homeless. Because I'm hungry. 'Oh, do sit down!' they say then sneak out and call the cops. What do you make of that? All I ever ask for is a roof over my head. Nothing more. I'm a good fighter, me. I fought all my life. Some, some, shall we call him a gentleman, some gentleman, who has never fought once, not even once, takes me by the collar of my shirt. (*He roars suddenly.*) 'What you doing that for?' I ask him. And turn. Look at him. I just need to look at him and I break his collarbone.

*He picks up the wine glass.*

Cheers.

*They drink.* **Smith** *eats.*

**Trueman**    It's in the news again today. Every day. It's entirely impossible to even look at the news nowadays. Another fire. And it's the same story. Exactly the same story. Another salesman. I'm telling you. Another door-to-door salesman asks for shelter for the night. Next morning. The whole house burns down. I mean. In a way I can understand why people are a little suspicious.

*He shows* **Smith** *the newspaper.*

**Trueman**    Here. Have a look.

*He puts the paper down by* **Smith***'s food.*

**Smith**    I've read it.

**Trueman**    The whole town.

*He finds the appropriate story in the paper.*

Here. Look.

**Smith** *eats and reads the paper and drinks his wine.*

**Smith**    Is this Beaujolais?

**Trueman**    Yes. It is.

**Smith**    It's too chilled. Should warm it up a bit.

*He reads the article.*

'It appears that the fire was planned and carried out in exactly the same way as last time.'

*The two look at one another.*

**Trueman**    Incredible, isn't it?

**Smith** *puts the paper away.*

**Smith**    It's why I never read newspapers.

**Trueman**    Why?

**Smith**    Because it's the same thing every day.

**Trueman**    Yes. Of course. Quite. But. Well. That's true. That is true. But is stopping reading the newspapers really the only answer? I mean. In the end you still need to know what's going on.

**Smith**    Why?

**Trueman**    Well. So, you know what's going to happen next.

**Smith**    Whatever's going to happen next, Mr Trueman. Is going to happen. Yeah?

*He sniffs the sausage.*

No escaping judgement day is there?

*He cuts the sausage.*

**Trueman**    Isn't there?

**Anna** *brings in the mustard.*

**Smith**    Thank you so very much.

**Anna**    Will there be anything else?

**Smith**    Not today.

**Anna** *stays by the door.*

**Smith**    I love mustard, me. It's my favourite.

*He squeezes a lot of mustard out of the tube.*

**Trueman**    Why do you think there's no escaping judgement day?

**Smith**    It's just what they say, isn't it? It's an expression.

*He eats and reads the paper again.*

'Forensic experts believe that the fire was planned and carried out in exactly the same way as those fires last week.'

*He laughs once then refills his wine glass.*

**Anna**    Mr Trueman?

**Trueman**    What is it, Anna?

**Anna**    Mr Waits would like to speak to you.

**Trueman**    Waits? Now? Waits? Really?

**Anna**    He said –

**Trueman**    No. No way. Absolutely not.

**Anna**    He couldn't understand –

**Trueman**    What couldn't he understand, precisely?

**Anna**   He has a wife and three children –

**Trueman**   I said absolutely not and I meant absolutely not. No. No. Absolutely not.

*He stands up. He paces in impatience.*

Mr Waits! Mr Waits! Mr Waits should leave me alone. Good God he should. Mr Waits should learn to wait! Ha! Thank you very much! I have finished work for the day. Mr Waits! I don't feel guilty for sacking him you know? It's ridiculous. And nowadays. He can get state support. Can't he? There has never been an easier time in the history of humanity to be unemployed. Has there? No. No. No, there hasn't. Maybe he should get himself a lawyer or something? He can have that idea for free. I'll get myself one too. I mean please! Mr Waits has got it in him to afford a lawyer. Hasn't he? Seriously? Seriously?

*He calms himself down when* **Smith** *catches his eye.*

**Trueman**   Tell Mr Waits that I have a guest.

**Anna** *leaves.*

**Trueman**   I'm so sorry.

**Smith**   It's your home, Mr Trueman. You can do what you want in your own home.

**Trueman**   How is it? The sausage?

*He sits himself down and watches his guest eat.*

**Smith**   Who would have thought people would still do things like that? Nowadays?

**Trueman**   More mustard?

**Smith**   Humanity.

*He screws the top back on the mustard.*

All I'm saying is that you would never just take a man by his collar, Mr Trueman, and throw him out on the street. In the rain. Would you? And that, Mr Trueman, that is what we need. Humanity.

*He takes the bottle and pours himself more wine.*

**Trueman**   I wouldn't want you to think, Mr Smith, that I'm a cruel person. That I'm inhumane.

**Smith**   Mr Trueman!

**Trueman**   That's what Mrs Waits called me.

**Smith**   If you were inhumane and cruel, Mr Trueman, then you wouldn't give me a bed for the night, would you?

**Trueman**   Now. I don't think I –

**Smith**   Even if it's only a bed in your attic.

*He puts down the glass.*

That's better. The wine. The temperature I mean. It's warmed up a little.

*The doorbell rings.*

Is that the police?

**Trueman**   My wife would really not –

**Smith**   Huh.

*The doorbell again.*

**Trueman**   Alright then. But under one condition. Please. Mr Smith. No noise. My wife has a heart condition you see.

*We can hear women's voices outside and* **Trueman** *gestures to* **Smith** *to help him. They take the tray and the glasses and the bottle and they tiptoe out right to where the* **Chorus** *is.*

**Trueman**   Excuse me.

**Trueman** *climbs over the* **Chorus**.

**Smith**   Sorry.

**Smith** *climbs over the bench too.*

**Smith** *and* **Trueman** *disappear.* **Bobsy** *comes in with* **Anna**. **Anna** *takes her things from her.*

**Bobsy**   Where's my husband? You know, Anna, we're not a narrow-minded middle class couple of prudes. We don't mind if you have a boyfriend. I just don't want you to hide him in the house.

**Anna**   Mrs Trueman. I don't have a boyfriend.

**Bobsy**   Then whose bicycle is that? That rusty old bicycle by the front door?

It scared me to death.

*The Attic*

**Trueman** *turns a light on and reveals the attic.*

*He gestures to* **Smith** *that he should enter.*

*The men whisper.*

**Trueman**   Here's the light switch. If you get cold . . . there's an old, what, a sheepskin rug, I think. Somewhere. I think. There used to be. But please. Quietly. For God's sake! Take your shoes off!

**Smith** *puts the tray down and takes off his one of his shoes.*

**Trueman**   Mr Smith. Joseph.

**Smith**   Mr Trueman?

**Trueman**   You do promise me. Don't you?

**Smith**   Promise you what?

**Trueman**   That you're not an arsonist.

**Smith** *laughs.*

**Trueman**   For God's sake please be quiet.

**Trueman** *nods goodnight and closes the door.*

**Smith** *takes off his other shoe.*

*The Living Room*

**Bobsy** *has heard a noise. She is frozen stock still. Listening. She looks terrified.*

*Then, with sudden relief, she turns to the audience.*

**Bobsy**   My husband, Godfrey, promised me that he would go up to the attic himself every night, personally, to check that there's no arsonist up there. I am so grateful to him. Without him I'd lie awake all night worrying.

*The Attic*

**Smith**, *now in his pants and socks, goes to the light switch, and switches off the light.*

*The* **Chorus** *steps into the light.*

**Chorus**
> DON'T LET THE FEAR OF FIRE
>
> TROUBLE YOUR SLUMBERING
>
> SLEEP LIKE A BABY
>
> ONCE THE LIGHT GOES OUT
>
> LEAVE ALL THAT CARE TO US
>
> SHARP-EYED AND WATCHFUL
>
> THERE'S NO NEED FOR YOU TO BE
>
> OUT AND ABOUT
>
> SLEEP WHEN WE TELL YOU TO
>
> SAFE IN THE KNOWLEDGE THAT
>
> ALL OF THE DANGERS ARE
>
> UNDER CONTROL
>
> SAFE IN THE ARMS OF THE
>
> HOMES YOU WORKED HARD FOR
>
> YOUR PROPERTY GUARDED
>
> SECURELY AS GOLD

**Bobsy** *appears. She is in her dressing gown.*

**Bobsy**    I heard a noise. It was like a horrible coughing.
Godfrey! Did you hear that?

*There is the sound of coughing.*

There it is again!

*Then the sound of snoring.*

That man! He could sleep through anything.

**Chorus**
  WE'RE ON THE ROOFTOPS

  AND OUR EYES ARE TRAINED TO FIND

  THE SLIGHTEST SPARK THAT COULD

  THREATEN YOUR REST

  WE ARE YOUR GUARDIANS

  AND YOU CREATED US

  HOW COULD YOU NOT HAVE

  CREATED THE BEST

  DON'T WORRY

  SLEEP SOUNDLY

  STAY QUIET AND

  MAKE NO FUSS

  ALL OF THIS BURDEN IS

  SHOULDERED BY US

  LOOK AS THE DAWN ARRIVES

  UNBURNED FOR ONE MORE NIGHT

  CITY SURVIVING

  BECAUSE WE ARE HERE

  ALL HAIL THE FIREFIGHTERS

WE ARE THE BEST OF US

VIGILANT GUARDIANS

OF ALL WE HOLD DEAR

**Scene Two**

*The Living Room*

**Trueman** *stands in his coat. He is wearing a hat. He is holding a leather briefcase. He is drinking a coffee.*

*He calls to someone off stage.*

**Trueman**    I'm not going to tell you again! He's not an arsonist.

**Bobsy** *(off)*    How do you know?

**Trueman**    Because I asked him myself! Don't you people ever do anything apart from sit there worrying about things? It'll drive you out of your mind you know. All your talk of fire all the time.

**Bobsy** *comes in. She has a bottle of milk.*

**Trueman**    You're losing your minds.

**Bobsy**    Don't shout at me.

**Trueman**    I'm not shouting at you, Bobsy. I'm shouting at the world.

*She pours milk into his coffee.*

I have to go.

*He sips his coffee. It's boiling hot.*

What good does it do you thinking that everybody is an arsonist? You need to have a little bit of faith, Bobsy. A little bit of faith.

*He checks the time.*

**Bobsy**   You're too trusting. That's your problem. I'm not like you. You open up your heart to everybody while I lie awake all night worrying. I'll take him his breakfast, Godfrey, but then I'm kicking him out.

**Trueman**   Fine. You do that.

**Bobsy**   I'll be a picture of kindness about it. I won't upset anybody.

**Trueman**   Good thinking.

*He puts his cup down.*

I have a meeting about employment law. And Mr Waits. With my solicitor.

*He gives* **Bobsy** *a perfunctory little kiss. And just at that moment* **Smith** *enters. He is wrapped in the sheepskin rug. The couple don't see him at first.*

**Bobsy**   Godfrey. Why did you sack Mr Waits?

**Trueman**   Because he had become expendable. I don't need him anymore.

**Bobsy**   But you've always been so pleased with him.

**Trueman**   And now he's trying to exploit that. He asked for a share in what he called his invention. And Waits knows perfectly well that what we are selling is a commercial act of unapologetic exploitation. Hair Replacement System? You may as well massage urine into your big fat bald head.

**Bobsy**   Godfrey!

**Trueman**   It's true!

*He checks he has everything in his briefcase.*

I *have* been too trusting, darling, you're absolutely right. Of Mr Waits. Well, not any longer. I'd rather squeeze the very life out of him than cast my eyes on him one more time.

*He's about to leave when he sees* **Smith**.

**Smith**    Good morning. Mr Trueman. Mrs Trueman.

**Trueman**    Mr Smith.

*He holds his hand out to him.*

**Smith**    Joe. Please.

**Trueman**    My wife will sort you out, Mr Smith. I need to go. Unfortunately. But – It's been a great pleasure to have you here. I wish you so much luck.

**Trueman** *leaves.*

**Smith**    Yes! Good luck to you too, Godfrey. Good luck to you too!

**Bobsy** *stares at him.*

**Smith**    That's his name, isn't it? Godfrey?

**Bobsy**    How did you sleep?

**Smith**    Yes. Thank you. I was terribly cold. But I managed to find this, this, this sheepskin. Which is . . . It reminds me of my childhood days in the incendiary. But. Yes. Well. I'm used to the cold.

**Bobsy**    Your breakfast is ready.

**Smith**    Mrs Trueman!

*She points the chair out to hm.*

I can't accept breakfast on top of everything else!

*She pours him a cup of coffee.*

**Bobsy**    I'd eat up if I were you. You've got a long way to go.

**Smith**    What do you mean?

*She reiterates her idea that he sits at the table.*

**Bobsy**    Soft boiled egg?

**Smith**    Two please.

**Bobsy**    Anna!

**Smith**    Thing is, Mrs Trueman, I already feel really at home here. I feel so free.

*He sits down.*

**Anna** *has entered.*

**Bobsy**    Two soft boiled eggs please, Anna.

**Anna**    Coming right up.

**Smith**    Three and half minutes.

**Anna**    Righto.

**Anna** *heads to leave.*

**Smith**    And Miss.

**Anna** *stops at the doorway.*

**Smith**    Morning!

**Anna**    Good morning.

*She leaves.*

**Smith**    The way she looks at me. I swear. If it was down to her, I'd be out on my uppers in the pouring rain.

**Bobsy** *pours coffee.*

**Bobsy**    Mr Smith.

**Smith**    Mrs Trueman!

**Bobsy**    Can I speak frankly?

**Smith**    You're shaking.

**Bobsy**    Mr Smith.

**Smith**    What's on your mind?

**Bobsy**    Have some cheese.

**Smith**    Oh. Thank you.

**Bobsy**    And some jam.

**Smith**    Oh. Thank you.

**Bobsy**    And some honey!

**Smith**    Keep it coming, Mrs Trueman, keep it coming!

*He leans back and starts eating his sandwich. He's listening to her.*

What's the matter Mrs Trueman?

**Bobsy**    Well. To be honest, Mr Smith –

**Smith**    Joe. Please.

**Bobsy**    To be honest.

**Smith**    You want shot of me?

**Bobsy**    No, Mr Smith! I wouldn't say that. I wouldn't put it that way!

**Smith**    How would you put it?

*He takes some more cheese.*

I love a bit of Tilsiter me. It's my favourite.

*He leans back. Ready to hear her story.*

So. Mrs Trueman. You think I'm an arsonist.

**Bobsy**    No! No, I don't! When did I say that? That was the last thing I thought, Mr Smith. The last thing I would ever want to do is offend you. I swear. This is nothing at all to do with anything you've done.

**Smith** *puts down his cutlery.*

**Smith**    I understand. I have the manners of a huge pig.

**Bobsy**    No. Mr Smith. It's nothing to –

**Smith**    I'm one of those people who makes a horrible noise when they eat, aren't I?

**Bobsy**    No. That's not true.

**Smith**    That's what they all used to say about me. In the
orphanage. They said. 'Oy! Smithy! Stop making that
fucking horrible noise when you eat, you fucking pig!'

*She takes the coffee pot to pour more coffee.*

**Bobsy**    Oh God no. That's not what I meant at all –

*He puts his hand over his cup.*

**Smith**    No. No. Time for me to go.

**Bobsy**    Mr Smith.

**Smith**    Time for me to take my leave.

**Bobsy**    One more coffee?

*He shakes his head and turns away melodramatically.*

Half a cup.

*Another shake. Another turn.*

You can't go like this. Oh God. I couldn't face it. I never once
wanted to upset or offend you. God. Or say that you made a
noise when you ate!

*He stands up.*

Did I offend you?

*He folds his napkin.*

**Smith**    There's nothing you can do about my incorrigible
lack of manners. My father worked in the power station. He
manned the incendiary. Where on earth would I get
manners from? I was too hungry for manners. Too freezing
cold. Mrs Trueman. I understand how it is. I have no
manners. No education. No culture.

**Bobsy**    I'm so sorry.

**Smith**    I'll be on my way.

**Bobsy**    Where will you go?

**Smith**    I'll head out into the rain.

**Bobsy**    Oh God.

**Smith**    I don't mind the rain. I'm used to it.

**Bobsy**    Mr Smith. Don't look at me like that. Your father worked in a power station. I can see how that would mean you had a horrible childhood.

**Smith**    It wasn't at all horrible, Mrs Trueman.

*He looks down. Twiddles his fingers.*

It wasn't. At least the first seven years weren't. Until my mother died.

*He turns away from her and wipes his eyes.*

**Bobsy**    Joe. Oh Joe!

**Anna** *comes in. She has two soft boiled eggs.*

**Anna**    Can I get you anything else?

*Nobody answers her. So, she leaves again.*

**Bobsy**    I'm not sending you away, Joe. I never said I was. When did I say that? You got it all wrong, Mr Smith. It's awful. How can I make you believe me?

*She dares herself to grab his arm.*

Come on. Joe. Have some breakfast.

**Smith** *sits down at the table again.*

**Bobsy**    What must you think of me? It never even crossed my mind that you made a noise, what? A noise? When you eat? Honestly! And if I had. Well. I wouldn't jump to any conclusions about what such noises meant about your personality! Mr Smith, you have to know that I am not that kind of person at all!

*He cuts the top off his egg.*

**Smith**    God bless you, Mrs Trueman.

**Bobsy**    Have some salt.

*He opens up the egg.*

**Smith**    You're so right, Mrs Trueman. You didn't kick me out at all. You didn't send me away. None of that. I can only say sorry, Mrs Trueman. I misunderstood the situation completely.

**Bobsy**    How's the egg?

**Smith**    It's a bit soft as it goes. Do excuse me.

*He picks up the egg and sucks it out of the shell in one mouthful.*

What was it you did want to say? When you said you wanted to speak frankly.

**Bobsy**    Yes. What was it?

*He takes the top off his second egg.*

**Smith**    Cheers.

*He eats the second egg.*

My mate Moll. She always says that human compassion has completely disappeared. There are no good people anymore. With all the racism! There's no human beings left. That's why the world's gone to hell in a handbag. Handbasket! Handcart!

*He salts the egg.*

Wait till she hears this story. If she saw a breakfast like this! Her eyes would pop out of her bleeding head. To Moll!

*The doorbell goes.*

Maybe this is her!

*The doorbell goes again.*

**Bobsy**    Who is she? This Moll?

**Smith**    She's a woman of culture is who she is, Mrs
Trueman. You wait and see. She worked at the Metropol.
She was the waiter there. Before it burned down.

**Bobsy**    It burned down?

**Smith**    She was the head waiter come to think of it.

**Anna** *comes in.*

**Bobsy**    Who is it, Anna?

**Anna**    It's a lady.

**Bobsy**    Is it? What does she want?

**Anna**    She's actually from the insurance company. She has
to inspect the fire safety on the house.

**Bobsy** *stands up.*

**Anna**    She's wearing a remarkable blue overcoat.

**Bobsy** *and* **Anna** *leave.* **Smith** *pours more coffee.*

**Smith** (*grinning to himself, and then grinning to the audience*)
It's Moll!

*The* **Chorus** *returns.*

**Chorus**
TWO OF THEM. ALREADY.

WE WERE GETTING SUSPICIOUS.

THE RUSTY BICYCLES.

THEY MUST BELONG TO SOMEBODY.

BUT WHO?

ONE SINCE YESTERDAY.

ANOTHER TODAY.

OH GOD!

AND IT'S NIGHT AGAIN. TIME FOR US TO GO TO
WORK.

*A clock outside strikes.*

JUMPING AT THE

SHADOWS AS THEY PASS

THE TIMID ONES SEE

DANGER WHERE THERE'S NONE

INVENTED MONSTERS LURKING

ON THE EDGE OF VISION, THAT

OBSCURE THE VIEW OF TRULY EVIL ONES

THE PROBLEM WITH A FEAR-OBSTRUCTED VIEW

IS THE FEARFUL OBSTACLES

YOU CAN'T SEE THROUGH

SO SELF-DELUDING HOPE

BRINGS DOWN ALL YOUR DEFENCES

WHEN REAL EVIL COMES

CREEPING AROUND YOU

YOU GET SO TIRED OF

JUMPING OUT YOUR SKIN

THAT WHEN TRUE MONSTERS COME

YOU MAKE THEM GUESTS

AND BY THE TIME YOU REALISE

YOU MIGHT HAVE LET IN EVIL

ALL YOU'VE GOT

IS HOPING FOR THE BEST

COS YOU'RE NOT THE KIND OF

COWARD WHO FUCKS UP

IF YOU CHOOSE TO ADMIT THAT

YOU LOSE TOO MUCH

*The clock strikes again.*

OH GOD!

*The* **Chorus** *sits again.*


**Scene Three**

*The Attic*

**Smith** *is still in his fighting clothes.* **The Visitor** *has taken off her blue overcoat and is now only wearing a white vest.*

*They are in the process of moving barrels in the attic. The barrels are those tin barrels that are customarily built for storing petrol. They are moving everything as quietly as possible. Both have taken their shoes off.*

**The Visitor**    Shush.

**Smith**    And when he decides to call the cops?

**The Visitor**    Move forward a bit.

**Smith**    What do we do then?

**The Visitor**    Easy. Easy. Stop.

*They have rolled their barrel up to join a collection of others. The barrels have all been standing in the twilit dark.*

**The Visitor** *wipes her hands with a cotton rag.*

**The Visitor**    Why would he call the cops?

**Smith**    Why wouldn't he?

**The Visitor**    Because he'd get in as much trouble as we would.

*There is the sound of pigeons cooing and fluttering in the attic.*

It's daytime already. Fuck. We should get some sleep.

*She throws away the cotton rag.*

It's his own fault. Anybody with the amount of money he's got must be guilty. All of them. Nobody is innocent with a house like this. Stop worrying.

*There is a knock on the door.*

**Trueman**    Open this door! Open the door!

*The door rattles and shakes.*

**The Visitor**    Room service in this place is a bit feisty, innit?

**Trueman**    I told you to open the door and I want it opened now.

**Smith**    He's not normally like this.

*The door rattles and rattles.* **The Visitor** *puts her overcoat on. She doesn't hurry. She's agile. She fixes her appearance and wipes off the dust from her shoulders. Then she opens the door.*

**Trueman** *enters in his dressing gown. He doesn't see* **The Visitor** *who is obscured by the door.*

**Trueman**    Mr Smith.

**Smith**    Good morning, Mr Trueman. Good morning. I do hope the strange rumbling noises coming from up here all night didn't wake you up.

**Trueman**    Mr Smith.

**Smith**    I promise it won't happen again.

**Trueman**    I want you to get out of my house.

**Smith** *looks at him.*

**Trueman**    I said I want you to get out of my house.

**Smith**    When?

**Trueman**    Now.

**Smith**    Why?

**Trueman**    Because if you don't my wife will call the police. Or I will. I can call them just as well as she can, if I want to.

**Smith** *looks at him.*

**Trueman**    What are you just standing there for?

**Smith** *doesn't say a word. He picks his shoes up.*

**Trueman**    I'm not discussing this.

**Smith**    I didn't say anything.

**Trueman**    If you're assuming, Mr Smith, that I will let you get away with anything you want because you are, what, an actual professional fighter – the type that rumbles and rattles about all night –

*He points at the door.*

I told you to get out.

**Smith** *speaks to* **The Visitor** *who is still behind the door.*

**Smith**    I've never seen him like this before.

**Trueman** *turns round and is stunned into speechlessness by the sight of* **The Visitor**.

**The Visitor**    Hello. I'm Moll.

**Trueman**    What on earth is going on?

**Ironside**    Molly Ironside.

**Trueman**    How? What? Why are there two of you all of a sudden?

**Smith** *and* **Ironside** *glance at one another.*

**Trueman**    You didn't ask if you could bring a friend!

**Ironside**    See?

**Trueman**   What?

**Ironside**   I told you, didn't I? This is typical of you, Joe. You've absolutely no manners. You didn't even ask. What kind of behaviour is that? And now there are two of us all of a sudden!

**Trueman**   I am beside myself here.

**Ironside**   See?

*She turns to* **Trueman**.

**Ironside**   I did tell him.

*She turns to* **Smith**.

**Ironside**   Didn't I tell you?

**Smith** *is crestfallen.*

**Trueman**   I mean, what were you thinking? This is my house. Isn't it? Seriously? What were you thinking?

*There is no answer.*

**Ironside**   Well, answer the man when he's talking to you, Joseph?

*There's pause.*

**Smith**   Moll's my friend.

**Trueman**   And . . .?

**Smith**   We went to school together. Mr Trueman. We've known each other since we were little children.

**Trueman**   So?

**Smith**   I just thought –

**Trueman**   What?

**Smith**   I thought.

*A pause.*

**Ironside**  You didn't think. Is precisely my point. You didn't think anything.

*She turns to* **Trueman**.

**Ironside**  I completely understand, Mr Trueman. I mean everything he's said is true. But still. In the end.

*She shouts at* **Smith**.

**Ironside**  Do you seriously think that anybody should put up with this kind of nonsense from the likes of you? In their own home?

*She turns back to* **Trueman**.

**Ironside**  Joe didn't ask you at all?

**Trueman**  He didn't say a word.

**Ironside**  Joe.

**Trueman**  Not a word!

**Ironside**  And then you wonder why you get kicked out of everywhere you go.

*She shakes her head and laughs at* **Smith**.

**Trueman**  It's not funny! This is serious. My wife has a heart condition!

**Ironside**  See?

**Trueman**  She didn't sleep all night. Because of that . . . noise. That rumbling.

And. Never mind that. What the hell were you doing?

*He looks around the attic.*

What the bloody hell are those barrels doing there?

**Smith** *and* **Ironside** *look at a corner where there are clearly no barrels.*

**Trueman**  Here! Not there! Here. What's this?

*He knocks on the top of a barrel.*

**Smith**    It's a barrel. They're barrels.

**Trueman**    Where did these come from?

**Smith**    Do you know, Moll? Where all these barrels came from?

**Ironside**    It says they're 'imported'.

**Trueman**    Come on!

**Ironside**    It must say on them somewhere.

**Ironside** *and* **Smith** *start examining the barrels for an address.*

**Trueman**    I don't know what to say. What the hell were you thinking? My attic is absolutely packed full. To the ceiling. Absolutely packed full!

**Ironside**    Yes, it is!

**Trueman**    What were you doing?

**Ironside**    I think Joe got his maths wrong. Twelve by fifteen metres I told him.

And that's not right, is it. There's not a hundred square metres here, is there? I can't leave my barrels in the street is the thing, Mr Trueman. You'll understand that.

**Trueman**    I don't understand anything.

**Smith** *shows* **Trueman** *the address on one of the barrels.*

**Smith**    Here we are, Mr Trueman.

**Trueman**    What? I don't know what to say.

**Smith**    The address. Where they came from. Here.

**Trueman**    I have absolutely no idea what to say.

*He looks at the address.*

*Downstairs*

**Anna** *leads a* **Police Officer** *into the kitchen.*

**Anna**   I'll give him a shout.

*She leaves the kitchen. The* **Police Officer** *stays there.*

*In the Attic*

**Trueman**   Petrol?!

*Downstairs*

**Anna** *comes back into the kitchen again.*

**Anna**   And what was it exactly you wanted to speak to Mr Trueman about.

**Police Officer**   Business.

**Anna** *looks at him for a moment. Then leaves again. The* **Police Officer** *waits some more.*

*In the Attic*

**Trueman**   Is this true? Gentlemen? Is this true?

**Ironside**   Is what true?

**Trueman**   What it says here?

*He shows them the label.*

Who do you think I am? I've never known anything like it. Do you think I can't read or something?

*They look at the label.*

Seriously?

*He laughs at them as though they have been utterly taking the piss.*

Petrol!

*He interrogates them like prosecutor.*

What's really in these barrels?

**Ironside**   Petrol.

**Trueman**    Don't mock me. I'm going to ask you for the last time. Tell me what's in these barrels. You know as well as I do that you can't store petrol in an attic!

*He runs his finger over a barrel.*

Here. Smell that.

*He holds his finger under their noses.*

Does that smell like 'petrol' to you?

*They sniff his finger and look at each other.*

Does it?

**Ironside**    Yes, it does.

**Smith**    It does.

**Both**    Definitely.

**Trueman**    Are you actually both insane? Have you really filled my whole attic with barrels and barrels of petrol?

**Smith**    I mean. One thing, Mr Trueman. Neither of us are smokers.

**Trueman**    And to do it now. At a time like this. When every paper you read is full of warnings of the dangers. What were you thinking? My wife will actually have a heart attack when she sees what you've done up here.

**Ironside**    See?

**Trueman**    Stop saying that. You always say that! 'See?'

**Ironside**    You don't expect a woman to take this calmly do you, Joseph?

I know women. I know how they think.

**Anna** *calls up from downstairs.*

**Anna**    Mr Trueman! Mr Trueman!

**Trueman** *closes the door.*

**Trueman**    Mr Smith. Ms –

**Ironside**    Ironside.

**Trueman**    If you don't take these barrels out right now . . .

**Ironside**    Then you'll call the police.

**Trueman**    Yes! I will!

**Smith**    See?

**Anna** *calls up the stairs . . .*

**Anna**    Mr Trueman!

**Trueman** *whispers.*

**Trueman**    That is my last word on the matter.

**Ironside**    Which one?

**Trueman**    I am not putting up with petrol being stashed in my attic! I'm not putting up with it.

*There is a knock on the door.*

Just coming!

*He opens the door. A* **Police Officer** *comes in.*

**Police Officer**    Ah. Wonderful. Mr Trueman. There you are. You don't need to come down. I won't keep you long.

**Trueman**    Good morning!

**Police Officer**    Good morning!

**Ironside**    Good morning!

**Smith**    Good morning!

**Smith** *and* **Ironside** *bow.*

**Police Officer**    I'm afraid there's been something of an accident.

**Trueman**    Good God!

**Police Officer**    A gentleman whose wife claimed he worked for you, as an inventor no less, I'm afraid, well, last night he put his own head in an actual oven.

*He looks in his notebook.*

Mr Waits. Jonathan Waits. Resident of number 1, Ross Avenue.

*He puts his notebook away.*

Do you know anybody of that name?

**Trueman**    I –

**Police Officer**    Maybe it would be easier, Mr Trueman, if we spoke in private?

**Trueman**    Yes.

**Police Officer**    This is not a matter for your staff, is it?

**Trueman**    No. Of course.

*He heads to the door.*

If anybody is looking for me, gentlemen, I will be talking to the police.

You hear that? The police. I'll be right back.

**Smith** *and* **Ironside** *nod.*

**Police Officer**    Mr Trueman.

**Trueman**    Let's go.

**Police Officer**    What have you got in those barrels?

**Trueman**    What have *I* got?

**Police Officer**    If I can ask.

**Trueman**    Hair replacement oil.

*He looks at* **Smith** *and* **Ironside**.

**Ironside**    'ManBloom!'

**Smith**  'Finally men can breathe a sigh of relief!'

**Ironside**  'ManBloom!'

**Smith**  'Try it today!'

**Ironside**  'You won't regret a thing!'

**Both**  'ManBloom!'

*The* **Police Officer** *chuckles at this entertaining re-enactment and heads out of the door.*

**Trueman**    Did, he, er, die? Mr Waits?

**Trueman** *and the* **Police Officer** *leave.*

**Ironside**    What a charming man!

**Smith**    Told you, didn't I?

**Ironside**    He didn't mention anything about our breakfast.

**Smith**    Yes. That was, I have to say, uncharacteristically neglectful of him.

**Ironside**    You got the fuse wire?

**Smith** *reaches into his pocket.*

**Smith**    Really. Quite uncharacteristic.

*The* **Chorus** *rise again.*

**Chorus**
  YES – WE DID IT AGAIN

  THE CITY MADE IT THROUGH ANOTHER NIGHT.

  AND FRANKLY WE THINK WE DESERVE CREDIT
  FOR THAT

  BECAUSE WE WERE THE ONES WHO WERE

  WATCHING OVER YOU

  BUT – WE CAN'T DO IT ALONE

  YOU MUST ALSO KEEP YOURSELVES INFORMED

YOU NEED

TO KEEP UP WITH EVENTS

BUT DON'T LOOK FAR AWAY

AND FAIL TO LOOK CLOSE TO HOME

BECAUSE  – WE DID IT AGAIN

WE MANAGED TO KEEP EVERYBODY SAFE

WE ARE WARNING YOU THOUGH

IF EVERYTHING'S ON FIRE IT'S DOWN TO YOU

IT WON'T BE OUR FAULT

YOU GOT DISTRACTED BY THE OTHER SHIT

OF COURSE ALL THAT WE CAN DO REALLY

IS SHOW YOU WE ARE QUITE CONCERNED

CHORUSES DON'T POSSESS POWER

IT'S SOMETHING WE SIMPLY PERFORM

WE WATCH YOU STUMBLING AND CARELESS

INTO THE WIDE JAWS OF FATE

THE FIRE THAT YOUR COWARDICE STARTED

WE'LL NOTICE, BUT SADLY TOO LATE.

BUT ANYWAY, TRUEMAN'S HERE

LOOK AT HIM, UNWORRIED, OFF TO WORK

**Trueman**   Do you mind? I need to get past.

**Chorus**   We're not stopping you.

**Trueman**   Look. What exactly is going on here?

**Chorus**   We were about to ask you the same question.

Why don't you tell us what's going on?

**Trueman**    Nothing. There's nothing going on.

**Chorus**    So what about all that petrol?

In your fucking attic?

**Trueman**    Who said anything about petrol?

**Chorus**    We did.

**Trueman**    Well. Let me tell you. What it is, is absolutely none of your bloody business.

**Chorus**    We're not judging you.

But there are some civil and legal consequences.

**Trueman**    Are there really?

Are there really 'civil and legal consequences' because the last time I checked those petrol drums, which are only circumstantial evidence of any actual petrol by the way, those petrol barrels were on my private property.

**Chorus**    That's what we meant when we pointed out that –

They're in your fucking attic.

**Trueman**    Precisely. *My* attic. So maybe you can all piss out of my way and let me go and visit my solicitor?

**Chorus**    But what exactly are you going to do with them?

You've got to admit they're a little, what, flammable?

**Trueman**    I'll admit whatever the hell I want to admit, and I'll admit it to whoever the hell I want to admit it to because those barrels are on my private property.

**Chorus**

LOOK AT THE PROPERTY OWNER

WITH HIS UNBREAKABLE RIGHTS

WHO CARES IF HIS INACTION BURNS DOWN

ALL OF OUR HOMES IN THE NIGHT?

**Trueman**    I mean, come on. That's a bit cynical, don't you think?

**Bobsy** *enters.*

**Bobsy**    Excuse me. I'm so sorry. Can I just ask you something?

**Trueman**    I'm talking to the Chorus.

**Chorus**    Don't worry about us. This is all getting a little meta for our taste.

**Bobsy**    Make sure you get a large wreath. Lots of flowers. Ribbons. Don't worry about how much it costs.

**Trueman**    Good thinking.

**Bobsy** *leaves.*

**Trueman**    Right. Let's get this sorted.

**Chorus**    Thank God for that.

He's going to explain himself.

**Trueman**    Oh for God's sake be quiet!

I don't know how you lot manage to get up in the morning. There are literally arsonists round every corner as far as you lot are concerned. Has it ever struck you that maybe you should learn to trust a little more and suspect a little less?

**Chorus**    He sounds like he's deluding himself.

I don't think he means it.

I don't think he believes a single word he's saying.

**Trueman**    I'm just rather sick of living in fear all the time. And you are doing absolutely nothing to help with that sickness.

**Chorus**    He's trying to convince himself that it's not actually petrol.

**Trueman**    Alright. Okay. It's bloody petrol.

Does that make you happy? Is that better now? If I admit it's petrol and that I am actually terrified? Who does that help? Where does that get us? And, and you can choose to believe this or not. Last night, I was literally on the point of throwing them out.

**Chorus**   Oh that's okay then.

As long as he was literally on the point of it.

**Trueman**   I was.

**Chorus**   He was *going* to throw them out.

But he just didn't.

**Trueman**   I've got to think about my wife. She worries about these kinds of things.

**Chorus**   Oh! That makes sense.

We didn't realise you were embarrassed.

Imagine! That would have been fucking terrible.

I mean, it would be bad if the whole world caught fire.

But can you imagine how bad it would be if you were a bit too embarrassed to mention it at the time.

**Trueman**   Oh piss off.

**Trueman** *leaves*.

**Chorus**   Off he goes.

He can't even smell the petrol.

That's a metaphor. By the way.

For tolerating evil.

**Chorus**

THERE'S NOT TOO MUCH WE CAN DO, THEN

HE'S MUCH TOO FRIGHTENED TO SEE –

IF YOU'RE MORE SCARED OF CHANGE THAN
DISASTER

DISASTER'S WHAT IT HAS TO BE


**Scene Four**

*The Attic*

**Ironside** *is working alone, unwinding the cord from a reel and whistling to 'We'll Meet Again'. She interrupts her whistling to wet her index finger and holds out the pointing finger through the hatch in the roof to check the wind outside.*

*The Living Room*

**Trueman** *enters followed by* **Bobsy**. *He takes his coat off and throws down his briefcase. He lights a cigarette.*

**Trueman**    Just do what I tell you to do.

**Bobsy**    A goose?

**Trueman**    A goose.

*He takes his tie off. His cigarette still in his mouth.*

**Bobsy**    Why are you taking your tie off, Godfrey?

*He hands her the tie.*

**Trueman**    If I call the cops on them then they become my enemies. What use is that to anybody. Only takes one match and our whole house goes up in flames. Literally. What use is that at all? If I go upstairs, though. And I invite them to join us. And they accept my invitation.

**Bobsy**    What then?

**Trueman**    Well then, we're friends, aren't we?

*He takes his jacket off and hands it to his wife and leaves.*

**Bobsy**    Anna! I just want to confirm. You don't have the
evening off tonight.

We have friends. Coming for dinner. Lay the table for four
please, Anna.

*The Attic*

**Ironside** *sings 'We'll Meet Again'. There is a knock on the door.*

**Ironside**    Come in!

*She carries on whistling. Nobody enters.*

I said, 'Come in!'

**Trueman** *comes in. In his shirt sleeves. Cigarette in his hand.*

**Ironside**    Good morning, Mr Trueman!

**Trueman**    May I?

**Ironside**    How did you sleep?

**Trueman**    Absolutely terribly. Thank you for asking.

**Ironside**    There's a dreadful breeze.

*She keeps working. Unwinding the string.*

**Trueman**    I don't want to disturb you.

**Ironside**    Not at all. Mr Trueman, this is your house!

**Trueman**    I hate the idea of being an imposition.

*Pigeons coo in the roof.*

Where's our little friend gone?

**Ironside**    Joe? He's gone to work! Who would have
thought it? That lazy bugger! He got all upset about leaving
without his breakfast. I sent him packing. Sent him out to
find wood wool.

**Trueman**    Wood wool?

**Ironside**   To carry the sparks. Wood wool carries sparks further than any other material in my experience.

**Trueman** *laughs politely like* **Ironside** *has just told a rubbish joke.*

**Trueman**   What I wanted to say, Ms Ironside –

**Ironside**   You want to kick us out again?

**Trueman**   I was lying awake in the middle of the night. My sleeping pills all gone! It struck me. Up here. You don't have a toilet. No toilet at all!

**Ironside**   We piss out of the window into the gutter.

**Trueman**   Whatever you want to do, whatever suits you best.

It was just on my mind all night! You might want to have a bath! Or a shower! You must use my bathroom! Of course you must! I told Anna to lay out towels.

**Ironside** *looks at him. She shakes her head.*

**Trueman**   What? What's wrong?

**Ironside**   I can't for the life of me see where he put the fuse wire.

Have you seen the fuse wire anywhere?

*She looks around her.*

Don't worry about the bathroom, Mr Trueman. Seriously. We're used to it. There's no bathroom in prison either!

**Trueman**   Prison?

**Ironside**   Didn't Joe tell you that I've just come out of prison?

**Trueman**   No.

**Ironside**   He didn't say anything?

**Trueman**   No, he didn't.

**Ironside**   He only ever talks about himself, that one. There are so many people like him in this world. It exasperates me. In the end what can we do? He had such a hard upbringing. A very testing childhood. I didn't. I could have gone to university. My dad wanted me to become a lawyer. I chose not to.

*She goes to the hatch and talks to the pigeons.*

Coo! Coo! Coo!

**Trueman** *lights his cigarette again.*

**Trueman**   Ms Ironside. I have to ask you. I didn't sleep all night worrying about this. Tell me honestly. Is there really petrol in these barrels?

**Ironside**   You don't believe us?

**Trueman**   It's not that. I'm just asking.

**Ironside**   Who do you think we are, Mr Trueman? Seriously. Tell me honestly. What exactly do you take us for?

**Trueman**   I'd hate you to think that I couldn't take a joke. You've just got quite an unusual sense of humour.

**Ironside**   That's one thing we've learned.

**Trueman**   What?

What is?

**Ironside**   Joking is the third best disguise. The second best is sentimentality. Like when Joe tells his stories about spending his childhood sleeping in a power station, or the orphanage, or the life of a street fighter. All that. But the best disguise, I find, is always the absolute bollock naked truth. It's really strange. Nobody believes it.

*The Living Room*

**Anna** *brings in* **Mrs Waits**. *She is dressed in black.*

**Anna**   Do sit down.

**Mrs Waits** *sits down.*

**Anna**   But if you really are Mrs Waits then there's no point you being here. Mr Trueman wants nothing to do with you. He said –

**Mrs Waits** *stands up.*

**Anna**   Sit down.

**Mrs Waits** *sits down.*

**Anna**   I just wouldn't, you know, get your hopes up. For anything. At all.

**Anna** *leaves.*

*In the Attic*

**Ms Ironside** *stands and works.* **Trueman** *stands and smokes.*

**Ironside**   I don't know what's keeping Joe so long. It's not exactly very difficult to get wood wool. I hope he's not been caught.

**Trueman**   Caught?

**Ironside**   Don't sound so cheerful about it.

**Trueman**   When you say things like that, Ms Ironside, it's amazing to me. You and I have lived such different lives. It's like you come from another world altogether. 'Caught!' It's fascinating to me. A whole new world! Where I come from nobody gets 'caught!'

**Ironside**   People don't deal in wood wool in your world, do they, Mr Trueman?

That's a fairly obvious difference between our classes I would suggest, Mr Trueman.

**Trueman**   No! Not at all!

**Ironside**   Are you trying to suggest, Mr Trueman –

**Trueman**    I don't believe in 'different classes'. You must have noticed that about me, Ms Ironside. I'm not that old-fashioned in my thinking. Quite the opposite in fact. It rather worries me that, you know, the working class today spend all their time going on and on about class differences. Surely nowadays, Ms Ironside, whether we're rich or poor, fundamentally we're all human beings. All born from the same earth. Me and you, Ms Ironside, we're just human beings in the end, aren't we? Made of flesh and blood. I don't know, Ms Ironside. Do you smoke?

*He offers* **Ironside** *a cigarette, but* **Ironside** *shakes her head.*

**Trueman**    I'm not talking about, you know, equality! Of course not. There will always be some people who are worth more than other people because they are better than those people. Thank God! But I don't know why we can't just shake hands and get on with one another. A little bit of good will, a little bit of hope. A little . . . And then everything would be so much calmer. So much more peaceful. A bit of peace hurt nobody did it. The rich or the poor?

**Ironside**    Can I speak frankly, Mr Trueman?

**Trueman**    Of course! Please!

**Ironside**    You're sure you won't mind?

**Trueman**    On the contrary. The franker the better.

**Ironside**    I mean. Frankly speaking, you *really* shouldn't smoke up here.

**Trueman** *gets scared. He puts his cigarette out.*

**Ironside**    I know it's not my place to make the rules in your house, Mr Trueman. But. You know what I mean –

**Trueman**    Of course I do.

**Ironside** *bends down.*

**Ironside**    There it is!

*She picks the fuse wire off the floor and blows it clean of dust before she attaches it to the string. She whistles 'We'll Meet Again' while she works.*

**Trueman**    Tell me. Ms Ironside. What is it you are actually doing up here? What is all this for?

**Ironside**    It's the fuse wire.

**Trueman**    The –?

**Ironside**    To make the fuse. This is the fuse.

**Trueman**    The –?

**Ironside**    You'd have thought there'd be more expedient methods nowadays, wouldn't you? Joe always says that. 'More expedient methods.' But there's not really. Or if there is, that's all your high-end military stuff and we don't have the budget for that kind of thing. High-end militaristic arsenal is really terribly expensive nowadays. I guess it has to be. For international warfare. Only the best will do.

**Trueman**    It's a fuse.

**Ironside**    A detonating fuse.

*She hands the end of the string to* **Mr Trueman**.

**Ironside**    Could you hold this end, Mr Trueman. While I measure? Would you mind awfully?

**Trueman** *holds the string*.

**Trueman**    I mean. All jokes aside, mate.

**Ironside**    Just a second!

*She whistles 'We'll Meet Again' and measures the fuse.*

Thank you, Mr Trueman. Thank you so much.

**Trueman** *suddenly bursts out laughing*.

**Trueman**    Now hold on just a second here! You can't take me for an utter buffoon! I mean. Really. You test the edges of people's humour. Don't you? You do. You really – You do. No wonder you get arrested all the time! If you go round making jokes like that. Not everybody has the same sense of humour as I do, chum, I'll tell you that for nothing.

**Ironside** No. We need to identify absolutely the right people to do this kind of work.

**Trueman** At my local, for example. Let me tell you. If you tried to tell them to see the good in people, they'd look at you like . . .! They see the whole world like it's Sodom and Gomorrah!

**Ironside** I can imagine.

**Trueman** Only last week I was press-ganged into making a donation to our fire brigade. I won't say how much I gave!

**Ironside** Ha! No. Don't.

*She lays out the fuse.*

In my experience the people who have no sense of humour, they're the ones who, well when everything kicks off they have no idea what to do. They don't know where to put themselves!

**Trueman** *sits down. On a barrel. He's sweating.*

**Ironside** What's the matter, Mr Trueman? You've gone all pale all of a sudden.

*She pats him on his back.*

It's the smell, isn't it? I can always tell when people aren't used to it.

The smell of petrol. I'll open a window.

**Ironside** *opens the door to let air in.*

**Trueman** Thank you.

**Anna** *calls upstairs.*

**Anna** Mr Trueman! Mr Trueman!

**Ironside**    Is it the cops again?

**Anna**    Mr Trueman?

**Ironside**    It's like we're living in a police state round here nowadays!

**Anna**    Mr Trueman!

**Trueman**    Just coming.

*He whispers.*

Ms Ironside. Do you like goose?

**Ironside**    Goose?

**Trueman**    Goose. Yes. Goose.

**Ironside**    Do I like it? Why?

**Trueman**    Goose. Roasted with chestnuts.

**Ironside**    Spot of red cabbage?

**Trueman**    Oh yes. I just wanted to say. My wife and I. Well. It was my idea really. We just thought. If you'd like. I'd hate to impose. But if you would like to come to dinner. You and Joe, Ms Ironside.

**Ironside**    Today?

**Trueman**    Or tomorrow if you'd prefer?

**Ironside**    Tomorrow? I don't think we're going to be here tomorrow. But we could do today, Mr Trueman. That would be lovely.

**Trueman**    Should we say seven o'clock?

**Anna** *calls up the stairs.*

**Anna**    Mr Trueman!

**Trueman** *gives* **Ironside** *an awkward hug/handshake cross.*

**Trueman**    Lovely.

**Ironside**  Lovely.

**Trueman** *leaves and stops in the doorway again. He gives a friendly little nod while also glaring at the barrels and the fuse.*

**Trueman**  Lovely.

**Ironside** *goes back to work. And back to whistling.*

*The* **Chorus** *comes forward. The scene has ended, after all. But just as they take their position there is a noise in the attic. Something has fallen over.*

*The Attic*

**Ironside**  You can come out, Professor.

*A third person crawls out from between the barrels. He is wearing a pair of spectacles. These mark his out clearly as an academic.*

You heard him. Me and Joe have been invited to dinner. You'll have to keep guard here. Make sure nobody comes in here for a smoke. Right? Not before it's time.

*The third person cleans his glasses.*

I do sometimes wonder, Prof, what on earth it is you're doing with us. You don't seem to enjoy the fires or the sparks or the beauty of a blazing flame. Or sirens. Those sirens which are always that little bit too late. Or the dogs barking. Or the smoke. Or the cries and the howls of the people. Or the ash.

*The third person puts his spectacles back on. He is silent. He looks serious.*

*She laughs.*

I'm a little worried you're with us for political reasons.

Are you a fucking activist?

*She whistles to herself for a short while without looking at the* **Professor.**

**Ironside**    I never liked your sort. Academics. You know that though. I told you that the first day I met you. There's no joy in academia. No comedy. All your peers are so driven by ideology. You're so fucking serious all the time.

*She continues to fiddle and whistle.*

**Chorus**

THE RED HOSE

SEPARATE FROM THE BLUE HOSE

NEXT TO THE PINK HOSE

COILED UP BY THE GREEN HOSE

THE BRASS PUMPS

POLISHED TIL THEY'RE GLEAMING

THE GAUGES

**Chorus Leader**    There's a terrible wind. Which is a bit unfortunate.

**Chorus**

WE'RE READY

EACH ONE KNOWS OUR FUNCTION

EACH ONE PRIMED FOR ACTION

WE'RE READY AND WE'RE WAITING

**Chorus Leader**    And the fire hydrants?

**Chorus**

WE'RE WAITING

WE'RE WAITING

WE'RE WAITING

WE'RE WAITING

**Chorus Leader**    We are ready.

*Downstairs*

**Bobsy** *comes in. She is carrying a goose. The* **Professor** *is with her.*

**Bobsy**   Yes. I know. I understand, Professor. But my husband. Yes, I know it's urgent. Professor. It is urgent. I know. I will tell him.

*She leaves the* **Professor** *in the doorway and steps to the front of the stage.*

**Bobsy**   My husband ordered a goose. And look. Here it is. A goose. And now I'm meant to, what? Roast it?

Just so that we can get all chummy with our friends in the attic.

*The church bells ring.*

It's Saturday night. You can hear the bell. I have the strangest feeling.

It's silly. A hunch. It just won't go away. That these bells may be ringing in our city for the very last time.

**Trueman** *calls for* **Bobsy**.

**Bobsy**   I have to admit one thing. I'm not sure if Godfrey is always right. He has made the point in the past, he's said 'Of course there are bad people in this world but if we make them our enemies then our Hair Replacement System is finished!' And he hadn't even got involved in local politics then.

**Trueman** *calls for* **Bobsy**.

**Bobsy**   It's always the same. I know my Godfrey. He's too good natured. He always is. It's the same now. Oh! He's just too sweet.

**Bobsy** *leaves with the goose.*

*The* **Chorus** *take their place.*

**Chorus**
WHO IS THIS WANKER

THIS SCRUFFY WANKER

PUSHING HER GLASSES

DOWN HER NOSE

LOOKS LIKE SHE'S SPENT TOO

MUCH TIME IN DARK ROOMS

TOSSING OFF HER

ACADEMIC PROSE

SHE'LL WRITE AN ESSAY

EXPLAINING ARSON

SO THAT YOU FEEL IT'S

ALL YOUR FAULT

MAKE YOU FEEL GUILTY

WHILE YOU ARE BURNING

COS YOU DON'T GET

WHAT SHE'S ON ABOUT

YOU MIGHT SEE PETROL

YOU MIGHT SMELL PETROL

BUT SHE'LL EXPLAIN THAT'S

JUST AN IDEA

AND WHILE THE WORLD BURNS SHE'LL ANALYSE
IT

THOUGH THE FLAMES ARE

LICKING HER OWN FACE

**Professor**    Good evening . . .

**Chorus Leader**
MAN THE HOSES!

MAN THE PUMP!

MAN THE LADDERS!

*The firefighters run to their seats.*

**Chorus Leader**    Everybody ready?

*The **Chorus** shouts that they are ready from all sides.*

**Chorus Leader** (*to the audience*)    We are ready. Are you?


**Scene Five**

*The Living Room*

**Mrs Waits** *is still there. Outside a fire alarm rings extremely loudly.* **Anna** *sets the table and* **Trueman** *brings in two armchairs.*

**Trueman**    Because. As you can see, Mrs Waits. I just don't have the time. I have no time, Mrs Waits, to deal with the dead. Like I said to you. A couple of times now. I do think the best thing is to contact my solicitor.

**Mrs Waits** *goes to say something. She can't. She leaves.*

**Trueman**    Anna! I can barely hear myself speak, Anna. Close the bloody window!

**Anna** *closes the window. The ringing is muffled.*

**Trueman**    I think the words I used to describe tonight's dinner were 'simple' and 'cosy'. What is going on with these ludicrous candelabras?

**Anna**    We always light the candelabras, Mr Trueman.

**Trueman**    Simple and cosy, I said. There's no need to bloody show off! Look at these water bowls! Silver and crystal. A knife rest! Everything is silver and bloody crystal! What will they think?

*He starts gathering in the cutlery and putting it in his pockets.*

Look at me, Anna. I'm wearing my oldest jacket. And you, Anna – leave the carving knife. We'll need that. But otherwise. Get this silver away from here. I want our friends to feel at home. Where's the corkscrew?

**Anna**    Here.

**Trueman**    Haven't we got anything a little simpler than that?

**Anna**    In the kitchen. But it's a bit rusty.

**Trueman**    Perfect! Bring it here.

*He removes a silver wine bucket from the table.*

What's this for?

**Anna**    Wine.

**Trueman**    But it's silver!

*He stares at the bucket and then at* **Anna**.

**Trueman**    Do we always have that out here?

**Anna**    You need it, Mr Trueman.

**Trueman**    'Need'? What does it really mean to 'need' something? You know what we need? We need humanity. Friendship. Kindness. Take it away. And what the hell are these things?

**Anna**    Napkins.

**Trueman**    Are they made of silk?

**Anna**    They're all we have.

*He collects the napkins and puts them in the silver bucket.*

**Trueman**    You know, Anna, there are people all over the world, whole tribes of them, whole countries of them who live without any napkins at all. Human beings. Like us –

**Bobsy** enters. *She is carrying a large wreath.* **Trueman** *doesn't see her at first.*

**Trueman**    I don't even really know if we need a tablecloth.

**Bobsy**    Godfrey?

**Trueman**    We don't need anything that suggests any class difference exists anywhere in this city.

*He sees* **Bobsy**.

**Trueman**    What's that wreath for?

**Bobsy**    It's what we ordered. But they've only gone and delivered it here. I wrote down the address of the Waits' myself. In black and white. They've even got the message wrong.

**Trueman**    What's the problem with the message?

**Bobsy**    And the delivery boy said they sent the bill to Mrs Waits.

*She shows him the card.*

**Trueman** (*reads*)    'To our beloved Godfrey Trueman. Always remembered.'

Oh come on! That is unacceptable. This is absolutely out of the question.

*He goes back to the table.*

Bobsy, don't just stand there. You're making me nervous. Stop it. I've got too many things to deal with right now.

*She leaves with the wreath.*

Right. We'll get rid of the tablecloth. Anna! And don't forget. Dinner is not 'served'. Absolutely not. You come in without knocking. Very simply. Just put the food on the table.

**Anna**    I put the hot pan on the table?

*He takes the tablecloth away.*

**Trueman**    Look at that! Look at the difference. There is an immediate transformation! It casts an altogether different mood. A wooden table. Nothing more. It's like the Last Supper!

*He gives her the tablecloth.*

**Anna**    Mr Trueman. Should I really just bring the whole goose in the pan?

*She folds the tablecloth.*

What kind of wine would you like, Mr Trueman?

**Trueman**    I'll sort the wine out.

**Anna**    Really?

**Trueman**    Is there anything else we need to do?

**Anna**    Mr Trueman, I don't really have any non-work clothes. Like a simple sweater or whatever. Nothing that makes me look like I'm, you know, not a servant. But actually, am, instead part of your family.

**Trueman**    Borrow one of my wife's.

**Anna**    The yellow one? Or the red one?

**Trueman**    I don't care! Just something simple. Nothing fancy, just not your uniform. Okay? Is that pretty clear? And also, Anna, make sure everything isn't so bloody neat and tidy in here. Mess things up a bit will you? I'll be in the cellar.

**Trueman** *leaves.*

**Anna**    'Make sure everything isn't so bloody neat and tidy in here.'

*She throws the tablecloth into the corner and kicks it around a bit.*

Alright.

**Smith** *and* **Ironside** *come in. Both carrying flowers. They watch her kicking the tablecloth for a while.*

**Both**    Good evening!

*She leaves without looking at them.*

**Ironside**    Where's the wood wool?

**Smith**    The cops took it. It was a 'precaution'. Anybody who sells or owns wood wool without a police licence is arrested. It's the same throughout the whole country. A government edict.

*He combs his hair.*

**Ironside**    Have you still got matches?

**Smith**    No.

**Ironside**    Me neither.

**Smith** *blows on his comb.*

**Smith**    We'll have to ask yer man.

**Ironside**    Trueman?

**Smith**    Don't forget.

*He puts the comb away. Sniffs the air.*

Something smells good.

*The Cellar*

**Trueman** *is in the cellar. He is holding a bottle. Singing and laughter can be heard from upstairs. He comes to the front of the stage.*

**Trueman**    You can think whatever you like about me. But answer me this . . .

As long as they're singing. And drinking. They're not doing anybody any harm. Are they? This bottle is . . . if wine was a poem. It would be this wine here. If somebody had told me last week, seriously, in all honesty, hand on my heart, 'How long have you known they were the arsonists?' I'd say, 'It's not as simple as that. It's not like a sudden realisation. It's more gradual. It's "incremental" is what it is.' Without even realising. Out of nowhere. You're suspicious. I found myself, without anticipating it at all, suspecting both of them. You lot might have suspected them from the start. But honestly. My friends. What the hell would you have done if you were in my shoes? And when, precisely, would you have done it?

*He waits for an answer. There is none.*

I've got to go. I've got a party to throw.

*He exits quickly.*

**Scene Six**

*The Living Room*

*The dinner is in full swing.*

*The whole room is laughing at a joke* **Trueman** *just made. He is laughing more than anybody else.*

*He is gripping his bottle tightly.*

**Bobsy** *isn't laughing at all.*

**Trueman**    Lint! The lint from freshly washed cotton burns even faster. Seriously.

Can you believe that?

**Bobsy**    Why's that funny?

**Trueman**    But. Lint! Bobsy! You know lint, right?

**Bobsy**    Yes.

**Trueman**    That comes off. Cotton. When you wash. Oh you've got no sense of humour is your problem.

*He puts the bottle on the table.*

What are you meant to do, guys? Guys. What are you meant to do if somebody just doesn't have an actual sense of humour?

**Bobsy**    It's the only possible explanation why I'm not laughing at your jokes, isn't it?

**Trueman**    The point is. This morning Moll said she sent Joe to steal wood wool.

Wood wool, you know that stuff? And I ask him. I ask Joe. I said 'Joe, what does the wood wool actually do?' And he says. Well. He couldn't get any wood wool but he'd got some lint from some laundry that he'd collected. Yes?

**Bobsy**    I got that bit.

**Trueman**    Did you though? Did you really? And then Moll says, 'Brilliant! Lint burns even faster!'

**Bobsy**    Yes. I got that bit too.

**Trueman**    Did you?

**Bobsy**    I just don't see what's funny about it.

**Trueman** *gives up*.

**Trueman**    Let's have another drink guys.

**Trueman** *uncorks the bottle*.

**Bobsy**    Is that true, Mr Smith, you took all our cotton lint into your attic?

**Trueman**    Now this is funny, Bobsy. This morning. We even measured out the fuse wire together. Me and Moll.

**Bobsy**    The fuse wire?

**Trueman**    The detonation fuse.

*He fills their glasses.*

**Bobsy**    Can I ask, though. In all seriousness. Why are you doing all this?

**Trueman** *laughs*.

**Trueman**    'In all seriousness,' she says. 'In all seriousness.' Have you heard her?

In all seriousness, Bobsy, don't let them trick you. I told you. These guys have a sense of humour that's just. It's wild. People who move in different circles tend to have rather different senses of humour. That's one of my mottos, that is. The only thing now is for them to ask me for some matches!

**Smith** *and* **Ironside** *exchange glances.*

**Trueman**    Thing is. These two. They'll think I'm just all anxious and nervous and I've got no sense of humour and they can make me out to be a right muppet!

*He raises his glass.*

Cheers!

**Ironside**    Cheers!

**Smith**    Cheers!

**Trueman**    To our friendship!

*They down their drinks.*

Hey. Guys. In our house. Don't stand on ceremony. Tuck in.

**Smith**    I'm really full.

**Ironside**    Don't be silly. You can't be. You're not in the children's home anymore, Joe!

*She takes more goose.*

I have to say, madam. Your goose is just superb.

**Bobsy**    Thank you. I'm glad you like it.

**Ironside**    Roast goose! A glorious Pinot Noir! The only thing missing is a tablecloth!

**Bobsy**    Did you hear that, Godfrey?

**Ironside**    I mean, it's not essential. Just. A crisp white damask tablecloth. A touch of silver. Can't beat it.

**Trueman**    Anna!

**Ironside**    And the damask has flowers graced into it. But white flowers. Like they are made of ice! But. You know. It's not essential, Mr Trueman. Not essential at all. We didn't have a tablecloth in prison, I'll tell you that for nothing!

**Trueman**    Anna!

**Bobsy**    In prison?

**Trueman**    Where is that girl?

**Bobsy**    You've been in prison?

**Anna** *enters. She is wearing a bright red sweater.*

**Trueman**    Anna, bring the tablecloth back in here right now!

**Anna**    Right. Fine. Right away.

**Ironside**    And maybe a finger bowl if you have one.

**Anna**    Smashing.

**Ironside**    You might find it a little ridiculous, madam, but that's just the way with the working class. Look at Joe. He's told you all his stories about growing up in a power station and he's still never, in his life, seen a silver knife rest. You see this is a dream for somebody who's lived a life as botched as his has been. A table like this laid with silver and crystal.

**Bobsy**    Godfrey, we have all those things.

**Ironside**    I mean. It's not essential.

**Anna**    Whatever you want, guys! Coming right up!

**Ironside**    And napkins. Please. Bring some napkins.

**Anna**    Mr Trueman said –

**Trueman**    Now, Anna! Bring the bloody napkins!

**Anna**    Yes, sir.

**Anna** *leaves and brings everything back in.*

**Ironside**    I do hope you don't mind too much, madam. When you get out of prison, you see. You go for months. Months without culture or –

*She holds up the tablecloth to show* **Smith**.

**Ironside**    Do you even know what this is?

(*To* **Bobsy**.) He's never even seen one in his life.

(*To* **Smith**.) This is damask this is, mate.

**Smith**    So? What am I meant to do with it?

**Bobsy**    And where are our knife rests! Anna? Our knife rests!

**Anna**    Mr Trueman said –

**Trueman**    Bring the bloody knife rests, woman!

**Anna**    You told me to get rid of them.

**Trueman**    Now! Where are they for God's sake?!

**Anna**    In your left pocket.

*He reaches into his pocket and finds the knife rests.*

**Trueman**    All right. All right. Calm down.

**Anna**    I'm trying to stay calm, I promise.

**Trueman**    Calm down, dear!

**Anna** *roars at him and turns and runs away.*

**Ironside**    It's the wind. It does things to people.

*There is a pause.*

**Trueman**    Have a drink guys! Have another drink!

*They pour another drink. Say nothing.*

**Ironside**    There was a time, you know. When I ate goose every day. When I was a waiter. I used to love that job. Racing down those long corridors. Silver tray balanced in the flat of my hand. The only thing was. How did we clean our fingers after we'd eaten? That was the problem. Where else but in your own hair? Some people have crystal finger bowls. I had my own hair. I'll never forget that.

*She dips her fingers into a finger bowl.*

Do you know what trauma is?

**Trueman**    No.

**Ironside**    This was another thing they explained to me in prison.

*She dries her fingers.*

**Bobsy**   Can I ask you? Ms Ironside. Why were you sent to prison?

**Trueman**   You're not meant to ask that!

**Ironside**   I ask myself the same question. I was a waiter. Like I said. Nothing but a humble head waiter and then, for no reason at all, they confused me with one of the nation's leading arsonists.

**Trueman**   Huh!

**Ironside**   I was arrested in my own home!

**Trueman**   Ha!

**Ironside**   I was so completely shocked that I just played along with it.

**Trueman**   Hm.

**Ironside**   I was fortunate, madam. I had seven terribly sweet police officers.

They were ever so helpful. When I told them that I had to get to work and didn't have time for any of their 'getting-arrested-for-no-apparent-reason' shenanigans they told me that the reason I was arrested was that my hotel had been burned to the ground!

**Trueman**   Burned to the ground?

**Ironside**   Overnight. It turns out.

Right. I said. Right. That throws my shift rota into question, doesn't it?

In that case I probably do have time.

I passed it in the van on the way to prison. Our old hotel. I could see it through the bars on my little window. It was nothing but a burning edifice.

*She takes a big sniff of her wine and drinks and swills it like a connoisseur.*

**Trueman**    Then what happened?

**Ironside**    Hm?

**Ironside** *looks at the label.*

I thought I recognised it. The '49 Cave de l'Echanson!

Then what happened? Joe can tell you all about that. I was sitting in the waiting room fiddling with my handcuffs and who's brought in? This fella!

**Smith** *beams.*

**Ironside**    Cheers, Joseph!

**Smith**    Cheers, Molly!

*They drink.*

**Trueman**    Go on . . .

**Smith**    'Ooooh! Are you the arsonist?' They ask her. They offer her a smoke. 'Excuse me.' She goes, 'I'm terribly sorry but I don't seem to have any matches. I wonder, officer, although I know you do rather take me for an arsonist. Do you have a light?'

**Smith** *and* **Ironside** *laugh loudly. They relish this story.*

**Trueman**    Hm . . .

**Anna** *enters. She is wearing her cap and apron again. She hands a visitor's card to* **Trueman**. *He looks at it.*

**Anna**    He says it's urgent.

**Trueman**    I have guests.

**Smith** *and* **Ironside** *toast each other again.*

**Smith**    Cheers, Molly!

**Ironside**    Cheers, Joseph!

*They look at* **Trueman** *who looks back at the visitor's card.*

**Bobsy**    Who is it, Godfrey?

**Trueman**    Somebody describing themselves as a Professor of Philosophy open brackets Activist close brackets.

**Anna** *busies herself at the sideboard.*

**Ironside**    And what's that you've got there, my love? What are you hiding from us now?

**Anna**    It's a candelabra.

**Ironside**    Why are you hiding a candelabra?

**Trueman**    Bring it to me! This instant!

**Anna**    Mr Trueman said, to quote him –

**Trueman**    Come on! Right now!

**Anna** *puts the candelabra on the table.*

**Ironside**    What do you think, Joe? This lot have actual candelabras and they bloody hide them! But it's beautiful. It's silver. Real candles. Have you got any matches?

**Smith** *reaches into his pocket.*

**Smith**    No I don't.

**Ironside** *does the same.*

**Ironside**    Oh it's annoying. We've not got any matches, Mr Trueman. Neither of us.

**Trueman**    I do!

**Ironside**    May I?

**Trueman**    Allow me. I can do it.

*He lights the candles.*

**Bobsy**    What does the gentleman want?

**Anna**    I haven't got a clue. Makes no sense to me. He's totally silent. Says he's going to wait in the stairwell.

**Bobsy**    He won't come in and join us?

**Anna**    Says he needs to speak in private. He has something he needs to reveal.

**Bobsy**    What is it?

**Anna**    I can't make any sense out of it at all. He just keeps saying he wants to distance himself from any part of the matter.

*The candles on the candelabra are all lit.*

**Ironside**    It casts everything in such an extraordinary shade don't you think, madam? Candlelight.

**Bobsy**    Yes. It does.

**Ironside**    I love a touch of atmospherics.

**Trueman**    You know, Ms Ironside, I am so relieved to hear you say that.

**Ironside**    Mr Smith, I do wish you didn't make that awful noise when you ate.

**Bobsy** *whispers to* **Ironside**.

**Bobsy**    Leave him alone. The poor man.

**Ironside**    He has absolutely no manners, madam. I can only beg your pardon. It's awful. But I suppose there is nowhere he could have learned them. Raised in an incendiary. In a power station.

**Bobsy**    I know!

**Ironside**    From the children's home to the street fighting ring.

**Bobsy**    I know!

**Ironside**    From the street fighting ring to the theatre –

**Bobsy**    Well that I didn't know.

**Ironside**    His life was fated from the start. Fated from the start.

**Bobsy** *turns to* **Smith**.

**Bobsy**    I had no idea you were in the theatre.

**Smith** *gnaws on the goose leg and nods.*

**Bobsy**    Where were you based?

**Smith**    Backstage mainly.

**Ironside**    He's being modest. Thing about Mr Smith. He makes a tremendously convincing ghost. Have you ever seen him give his ghost?

**Smith**    Not now, Moll.

**Ironside**    Why not?

**Smith**    I worked in theatre for a week, madam. And then it burned to the ground.

**Bobsy**    It burned?

**Ironside**    He's so shy.

**Bobsy**    To the ground?

**Ironside**    Don't be shy, Joseph.

*She removes the tablecloth that* **Smith** *wore as a napkin and throws it over his head.*

**Ironside**    Do it!

**Smith**, *draped in the tablecloth, rises.*

**Ironside**    See. Doesn't he look like a ghost?

**Anna**    I am a little scared to be fair.

**Ironside**    Women, eh?

*She takes* **Anna** *in her arms. She holds her hands in front of her face.*

**Smith**    'Shall we?'

**Ironside**    That's a line from the play, Mrs Trueman. He was so clever. He learned all his lines in a week before the whole theatre burned down. Quite astonishing.

**Bobsy**    I wish you wouldn't keep talking about the fire.

**Smith**    'Shall we?'

**Ironside**    Well. I'm ready if you are.

*Everybody arranges themselves into an audience and gets ready for his performance.* **Ironside** *holds* **Anna** *close to her chest.*

**Smith**    EVERYONE LISTEN TO ME!

**Bobsy**    Godfrey?

**Trueman**    Quiet!

**Bobsy**    We saw this in Chichester, I think.

**Smith**    TRUEMAN! TRUEMAN!

**Ironside**    It is very good. His delivery.

**Smith**    TRUEMAN! TRUEMAN!

**Ironside**    You have to ask 'Who are you?'

**Trueman**    Me?

**Ironside**    Otherwise he'll get stuck on his lines.

**Trueman**    Okay! 'Who am I?'

**Bobsy**    No. You have to ask who he is!

**Trueman**    Ah! Right!

**Smith**    CAN'T YOU HEAR ME?

**Ironside**    No. Joe. Go again from the beginning.

*They reposition themselves to watch the next version of the performance.*

**Smith**   YOU LOT! TRUEMAN!

**Bobsy**   Oohh, is he, are you 'Death'? Maybe?

**Trueman**   Don't be ridiculous.

**Bobsy**   Well, who else is he?

**Trueman**   That's the point. You need to ask him who he is. He could be Hamlet's ghost couldn't he? Or a phantom guest. Or that, that guy, what's he called? The one from Macbeth . . .

**Smith**   WHO IS IT WHO CALLS FOR ME?

**Ironside**   Go on.

**Smith**   GODFREY TRUEMAN!!!

**Bobsy**   Go on. You ask him. He's talking to you!

**Smith**   CAN YOU HEAR ME?

**Trueman**   Who are you?

**Smith**   I AM THE GHOST OF . . . MR WAITS!!!

**Bobsy** *jumps to her feet and screams.*

**Ironside**   Stop that right now!

*She tears off* **Smith**'s *tablecloth.*

**Ironside**   You bloody idiot. You can't just do that!

Waits? That makes no sense. Waits was only buried today.

**Smith**   That was my point!

**Bobsy** *holds her hands in front of her face.*

**Ironside**   Madam. He's not really the ghost of –

*She shakes her head at* **Smith**.

**Ironside**   I don't understand how you can be so tasteless.

**Smith**    I couldn't think of anybody else.

**Ironside**    Waits? Of all the people you could have chosen.
An old and trusted employee of Mr Trueman. Imagine that.
Buried today no less. He's not even decomposed yet. He's
still as white as a sheet. As white as a tablecloth no less. Stiff.
Cold. But to try and make out that –

*She puts her arm around* **Bobsy**.

**Ironside**    I promise you, Mrs Trueman, this really isn't him
coming back to haunt you for the way he was treated.

**Smith** *wipes his brow.*

**Smith**    I'm sorry, Mrs Trueman.

**Trueman**    Let's all sit back down.

**Anna**    Is that the end of the show?

*There is a brief, slightly embarrassed, pause.*

**Trueman**    How about a cigarette guys?

*He offers round his cigarettes.*

**Ironside**    Such an idiot. Look. Even Mr Trueman's shaking
a bit. Thank you, Mr Trueman. Thank you so much.
Seriously. If you think you're funny when you know
precisely what's happened to Mr Waits. With him putting his
own head in the oven just because of the way our pal
Godfrey treated him. After fourteen years of loyal service.
This so-called Waits. And that is the thanks that –

**Trueman**    Let's not talk about any of this anymore.

**Ironside**    And that's how you thank them for the goose.

*They light their cigarettes.*

**Smith**    Maybe I could sing us all a song.

**Ironside**    I'm sorry?

**Smith**    'Three six nine, the goose drank wine'

*His singing becomes more confident and louder as the song goes on.*

'The monkey chews tobacco on the streetcar line'

**Ironside**    That's enough.

**Smith**    'The line broke, the monkey got choked'

**Ironside**    He's drunk.

**Smith**    'And they all went to heaven in a little rowing boat'

**Ironside**    Pay no attention to him miss.

**Smith**    'My mother told me

If I was goody'

**Trueman**    This is fun actually.

**Trueman** *and* **Smith**    'That she would buy me

A rubber dolly'

*Then everybody joins in.*

*And as they sing through the verses of the 'Clapping Song'.*

*They reunite their party again.*

*Having a whale of a time.*

*Until* **Trueman** *calls for their attention.*

**All**
   'My aunty told her
   I kissed a soldier
   Now she won't buy me
   A rubber dolly!'

**Trueman**    Brilliant! To my friends!

*They all toast.*

*In the distance sirens can be heard.*

**Trueman**    What's that?

**Ironside**    It's sirens.

**Trueman**    No. Seriously.

**Bobsy**    It must be the arsonists. The arsonists!

**Trueman**    Keep your voice down!

**Bobsy** *opens the window. The sirens come closer. Howling. Chilling the room to the bone. Then they pass.*

**Trueman**    Thank goodness they're not coming here.

**Bobsy**    Where are they going, do you think?

**Ironside**    Wherever the wind's coming from.

**Trueman**    Not here though. Thank the Lord.

**Ironside**    That's what we normally do. We get the fire brigade out to some neighbourhood out in the sticks and so later on when they try and get back they can't because the traffic's got so bad.

**Trueman**    Ha! Yeah!

I mean!

Come on, guys. Seriously.

**Smith**    No. Seriously. That's what we do.

**Trueman**    Stop messing. Ease up a bit. You can see my wife gets upset. She's white as a sheet.

**Bobsy**    And you aren't?

**Trueman**    Anyway. A siren is a siren. I'm not sure how funny I find the emergency services on the whole, guys. You've got to draw a line somewhere, don't you? I mean. There's a fire. An actual fire. Somewhere. Otherwise what would the fire brigade be doing haring out there?

**Ironside** *looks at her watch.*

**Ironside**    I'm afraid we need to get going.

**Trueman**    Already?

**Ironside**   I'm afraid so.

**Smith**   Or we'll all go to heaven in a little rowing boat.

*The sirens again.*

**Trueman**   Some coffee. Bobsy, pop some coffee on.

**Bobsy** *leaves.*

**Trueman**   And you, Anna. What are you standing there gawping at?

**Anna** *leaves.*

**Trueman**   Between us three. Enough is enough. My wife has a heart condition. Let's stop joking about the fires, yeah?

**Smith**   We're not joking, Mr Trueman.

**Ironside**   We are the arsonists.

**Trueman**   Yeah. Guys. Seriously –

**Smith**   Seriously.

**Ironside**   Seriously.

**Smith**   Why don't you believe us?

**Ironside**   Your house, Mr Trueman, is in a perfect location. You have to admit that. Start five fires in places like this. Around the peripheries of the power station. And the power station in this town is guarded so badly. When the wind's as strong as this.

**Trueman**   You're joking.

**Smith**   Mr Trueman! If you've known all along that we're the arsonists, you could at least admit it, yeah?

**Trueman** *looks like a scolded dog.*

**Trueman**   I don't believe that you are the arsonists though. Guys. You're not. It's not true. You're making me look like an idiot. It's not right. I don't believe you. The arsonists? You two?

**Ironside**    I'm afraid so.

**Trueman**    No. No. No. No.

**Smith**    Then who the hell do you think we are?

**Trueman**    My, my, my friends.

*They clap him on his back. And head away. Leaving him standing there.*

Where are you going?

**Ironside**    It's time.

**Trueman**    Seriously, guys. I swear to God. Come on!

**Ironside**    You swear to God?

**Trueman**    Yes I do.

*He holds his hand up as though swearing on the Bible.*

**Smith**    Moll doesn't believe in God any more than you do, Mr Trueman. You swear by whatever the fuck you want.

*They head to the door.*

**Trueman**    What can I do to make you believe how much I trust you?

*He blocks their exit.*

**Ironside**    Give us your matches.

**Trueman**    What do you mean? You want me to –?

**Ironside**    We've run out.

**Trueman**    You want me to –?

**Ironside**    If you really don't believe we're the arsonists.

**Trueman**    My matches?

**Smith**    As a token of your trust.

**Trueman** *reaches into his pocket.*

**Ironside**    Look at him. Hesitating.

**Trueman**    Okay. But. Not in front of my wife.

**Bobsy** *comes back.*

**Bobsy**    Coffee's on its way.

*A pause.*

Do you really need to go?

**Trueman**    Yes. My friends. It is unfortunate but – I hope
that the main thing is that you have come to feel that you are
– I don't want to waffle on – friends. We should just call each
other by our first names. Shouldn't we? Why don't we do
that?

**Bobsy**    Hm.

**Trueman**    I think we should raise a toast to our friendship
and our fraternity.

*He pulls out another bottle and a corkscrew.*

**Ironside**    Please, madam. Would you tell your dear
husband not to open another bottle. It's not really worth it
anymore.

**Trueman** *opens the bottle.*

**Trueman**    It is! Anything is worth it for you two, my friends.
Nothing is too much. If there is anything that you want.
Anything you need or desire or –

*He hastily fills their glasses.*

My friends! A toast!

*They raise their glasses.*

Call me Godfrey!

*He clinks* **Smith**'s *glass.*

**Smith**    Joe.

**Trueman**  Godfrey!

*He clinks glasses with* **Ironside***.*

**Ironside**  Moll.

*They down their drinks.*

It is a shame, Godfrey, but we do still have to go now.

**Smith**  It's a pity.

**Ironside**  Mrs Trueman.

*The sirens sound.*

**Bobsy**  It was such a lovely evening.

*Fire alarms ring out.*

**Ironside**  Just one more thing, Godfrey.

**Trueman**  What is it?

**Ironside**  You know exactly what it is.

**Trueman**  I said if there is anything . . .

**Ironside**  The matches.

**Anna** *enters with the coffee.*

**Bobsy**  Anna, what's going on?

**Anna**  The coffee.

**Bobsy**  You look so upset.

**Anna**  Outside. The sky, Mrs Trueman. From the kitchen window. The whole sky is on fire.

*And indeed, it is.*

*Burning and reddening as* **Smith** *and* **Ironside** *take their bows and leave.*

**Trueman**  Thank goodness it's not happening here. Thank goodness it's not happening here. Thank goodness –

*The* **Professor** *enters.*

**Trueman**   How can I help you, Professor?

**Professor**   I can't stay quiet about this for a second longer. I think this prepared statement will make everything perfectly clear.

*He takes a document out of his pocket and reads it.*

'I, the undersigned, who finds herself deeply shaken by the events which are currently underway and which also from a legal point of view can, it seems to me, only be characterised as a crime, offer the following clarification for the attention of the public.'

*The city is a roar of sirens outside as he reads his text. The words are drowned out by the noise of the alarms and the sirens and the fear, the dogs barking, the screams and the crackling oncoming sound of the fire. Only when they fade for a while do we hear the statement's close.*

'And in so doing I distance myself completely. I am not to blame.'

**Trueman**   Now what?

**Professor**   I think I have clarified my position on all things. I have said all I need to say.

*He takes off his glasses and puts them in his pocket.*

You see, Mr Trueman. I make no apology in considering myself what I choose to call an activist. A serious one. An honest one. I knew everything those two were doing in your attic. Everything. I was engaged. I was committed. But there was one thing I didn't understand. I didn't understand why they were doing it. They were doing it, Mr Trueman, purely and solely for fun. They lacked ideological rigour. They were doing it because it felt good. They were doing it because it made them laugh.

**Trueman**   Professor . . .

*The **Professor** walks away.*

**Trueman**    Hey. Professor. What am I meant to do with this?

*The **Professor** climbs into the auditorium and sits with the audience.*

**Bobsy**    Godfrey.

**Trueman**    He's gone.

**Bobsy**    Godfrey, what did you do? Did you do what I think I saw you do? Did you give them the matches?

**Trueman**    Yes. So. Why shouldn't I have done that?

**Bobsy**    Matches?

**Trueman**    Oh come on, Bobsy. If they really were the arsonists, do you honestly think they wouldn't have their own matches? Bobsy? Bobsy?

*The grandfather clock strikes.*

*There is silence.*

*The lights turn red.*

*The stage darkens. There is the sound of the fire alarms ringing out all over the city. Dogs bark. Sirens wail. Cars scream and howl their horns. Buildings fall. People scream. The fire crackles.*

*And then the **Chorus** steps forward.*

**Chorus**
WELL WHAT WAS THE POINT OF THAT?

SOME PEOPLE DIED AND SOME WERE SPARED

WE DIDN'T PUT OUT ANY FIRES

WE NEVER GOT TO USE THE HOSE

WE'D SO CAREFULLY PREPARED

**Chorus Leader**    That was the power station. The power station's on fire!

**Chorus**

BUT AT LEAST – DID SOMETHING CHANGE?

WE CAN REPORT THAT IT DID NOT

WE DIDN'T GET TO TRULY TEST

OUR OBSERVA-TI-ON-AL POWERS

ON THE STORY WE JUST GOT

THERE'S NO CONCLUSION TO BE DRAWN

THERE'S NO MORAL IN THE SHIT

SOME FUCKERS FOOLED

A WEAK-WILLED IDIOT

AND HE CHOSE TO SWALLOW IT

IF WE WERE FORCED TO FIND A TRUTH

IN THIS CHAOTIC ROUNDABOUT

DON'T WAIT FOR THE FIRE TO START

BEFORE YOU START TO THINK

THAT YOU SHOULD PUT IT OUT

SOME FOLK WILL TELL YOU THAT IT'S FATE

SOME CLAIM THAT THEY PREDICTED THIS

IT DOESN'T MATTER WHICH IS TRUE

BY THE TIME THE FIRE TAKES HOLD

THE FIRE IS ALL THERE IS

DEARY ME

DEARY ME

DEARY DEARY DEARY ME

*Light in the auditorium.*

9 781350 446410